Oceans of the World

The Arctic Ocean

By Lauren Gordon

Table of Contents

A Starfish Book

SEAHORSE PUBLISHING

Teaching Tips for Caregivers:

As a caregiver, you can help your child succeed in school by giving them a strong foundation in language and literacy skills and a desire to learn to read.

This book helps children grow by letting them practice reading skills.

Reading for pleasure and interest will help your child to develop reading skills and will give your child the opportunity to practice these skills in meaningful ways.

- Encourage your child to read on her own at home
- Encourage your child to practice reading aloud
- Encourage activities that require reading
- Establish a reading time
- Talk with your child
- Give your child writing materials

Teaching Tips for Teachers:

Research shows that one of the best ways for students to learn a new topic is to read about it.

Before Reading

- Read the "Words to Know" and discuss the meaning of each word.
- Read the back cover to see what the book is about.

During Reading

- When a student gets to a word that is unknown, ask them to look at the rest of the sentence to find clues to help with the meaning of the unknown word.
- Ask the student to write down any pages of the book that were confusing to them.

After Reading

- Discuss the main idea of the book.
- Ask students to give one detail that they learned in the book by showing a text dependent answer from the book.

The Arctic Ocean

There are five oceans on Earth.
One is the Arctic Ocean.

The Arctic Ocean is located near Earth's **North Pole**.

It touches the continents of North America, Europe, and Asia.

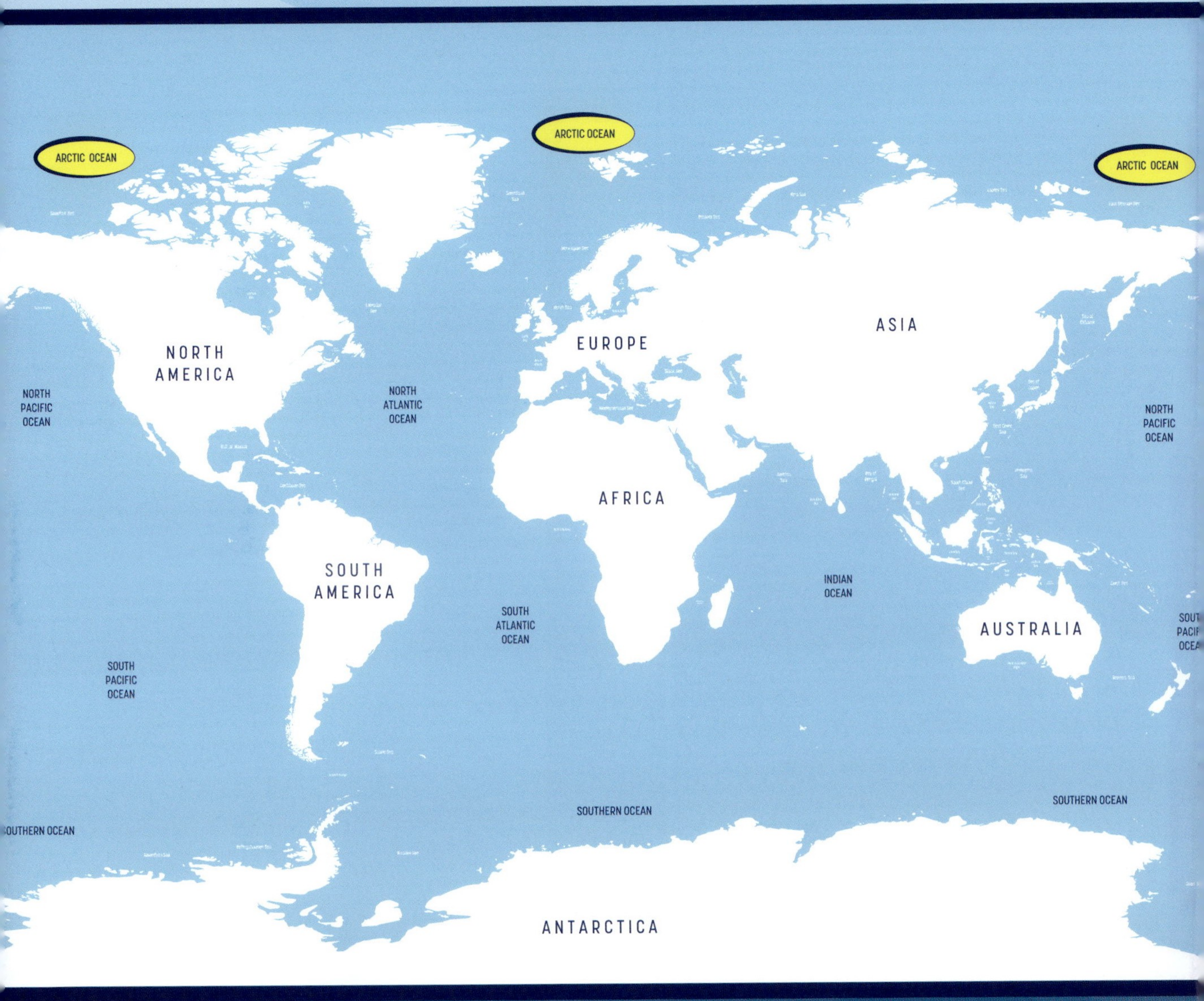
ARCTIC OCEAN
ARCTIC OCEAN
ARCTIC OCEAN
NORTH AMERICA
EUROPE
ASIA
NORTH PACIFIC OCEAN
NORTH ATLANTIC OCEAN
NORTH PACIFIC OCEAN
AFRICA
SOUTH AMERICA
INDIAN OCEAN
SOUTH ATLANTIC OCEAN
AUSTRALIA
SOUTH PACIFIC OCEAN
SOUTHERN OCEAN
SOUTHERN OCEAN
SOUTHERN OCEAN
ANTARCTICA

Most of the Arctic Ocean is covered by ice.

Each autumn, large parts of the Arctic Ocean freeze.

Most of an iceberg is hidden. Only the tip can be seen above water.

The Arctic Ocean has many **icebergs**.

Icebergs may break away from **glaciers** and float out to sea.

The Arctic Ocean got its name from the Greek word *arktos*, which means "bear."

Polar bears live in and around the Arctic Ocean.

The Arctic Ocean is the world's smallest ocean.

It is about the same size as one and a half United States of Americas put together.

Arctic Ocean
United States

Compared to other oceans on Earth, the Arctic Ocean is the **shallowest**.

The average depth is just above 3,000 feet (900 meters).

The Arctic Ocean is the coldest ocean in the world.

Arctic seals, walruses, and whales have a layer of **blubber** to help them survive in cold waters.

A beluga whale's thick skin, extra fat, and small fins help it survive in icy Arctic water.

Some Arctic animals have white coats only during the winter months.

Some animals that live near the Arctic Ocean are white.

This **camouflage** helps them hide in ice and snow.

The Arctic Ocean is in danger.

Its waters are warming, and less ice forms each year.

Many Arctic animals depend on ice for hunting, traveling, and shelter.

Words to Know

blubber (BLUHB-ur): a thick layer of fat under the skin of a whale, seal, or other large ocean animal

camouflage (KAM-uh-flahzh): a disguise or natural coloring that allows animals to hide by making them look like their surroundings

glaciers (GLAY-shurz): slow-moving masses of ice found in mountain valleys and in polar regions

icebergs (ISE-burgs): large masses of ice that float in the sea

North Pole (north pohl): the most northern point on Earth, located at the top of Earth's axis

shallowest (SHAL-oh-uhst): least deep; measuring the smallest from top to bottom

Index

Comprehension Questions

1. True or False: The Arctic Ocean is one of five oceans in the world.
2. True or False: The Arctic Ocean is the coldest ocean.
3. True or False: White fur, blubber, and other adaptations help Arctic animals survive.
4. True or False: The Arctic Ocean is the deepest ocean on Earth.
5. True or False: The Arctic Ocean is named after the Greek word *arktos*.

Answers
1. True 2. True 3. True 4. False 5. True

About the Author

Lauren Gordon is originally from New York and now lives in Florida. She lives with her husband and two children. In her free time, she likes to read and spend time with her family.

Written by: Lauren Gordon
Design by: Jen Bowers
Editor: Kim Thompson

Photographs from Shutterstock.com: Cover and p.8 image ©2017 Romolo Tavani, backgound ©2012 Andrey_Kuzmin, water globe ©2012 zffoto; p.2 and throughout backgroud ©elic; p.3 and throughout background ©Aleksandra Bataeva, globes ©Designua; p.5 ©Pyty; p.7©2019 Risto Raunio; p.11 ©2020 Alexey Seafarer; p.13 ©2010 Jacek Fulawka; p.15 ©2019 Vojtech Jirka; p.17 ©2009 Christopher Meder; p.18 ©2016 Ondrej Prosicky, ©2018 JoannaPerchaluk; p.21 ©2020 PHOTOCREO Michal Bednarek

Library of Congress PCN Data
Oceans of the World / Gordon
The Arctic Ocean
ISBN 978-1-63897-450-5 (hard cover)
ISBN 978-1-63897-565-6 (paperback)
ISBN 978-1-63897-680-6 (EPUB)
ISBN 978-1-63897-795-7 (eBook)
Library of Congress Control Number: 2021953382

Printed in the United States of America.

Seahorse Publishing Company
www.seahorsepub.com

Published in the United States
Seahorse Publishing
PO Box 771325
Coral Springs, FL 33077

SEAHORSE PUBLISHING